Photography courtesy of
FRANK OCKENFELS 3 and MARK TUCKER

7777 W. BLUEMOUND RD. P.O.BOX 13819 MILWAUKEE, WI 53213

© 1992 The Sparrow Corporation./P.O. Box 5010 / 101 Winners Circle/Brentwood, TN 37024-5010
All Rights Reserved. International Copyright Secured.

For all works contained herein:
Unauthorized copying, arranging, adapting, recording or public performance is an infringement of copyright.
Infringers are liable under the law.

Visit Hal Leonard Online at
www.halleonard.com

Table Of Contents

Busy Man	97
Don't Let The Fire Die	127
For The Sake Of The Call	83
For Who He Really Is	24
Go There With You	120
Hiding Place	12
His Eyes	29
His Strength Is Perfect	41
I Will Be Here	54
Love You With My Life	60
More To This Life	46
My Turn Now	35
No Better Place	91
Run Away	19
Still Called Today	135
The Great Adventure	111
Treasure Island	74
Weak Days	6
What Kind Of Joy	104
When You Are A Soldier	66

Weak Days

Words and Music by
STEVEN CURTIS CHAPMAN
and JAMES ISAAC ELLIOTT

1. An-oth-er rain-y Mon-day, looks like I'm gon-na be late a-gain.
2. (The Spir-it) is so will-ing when all the fel-low-ship is so sweet. How

© 1987 Birdwing Music/Sparrow Song (Divisions of The Sparrow Corp.) and BMG Songs, Inc./Careers-BMG Music Publishing, Inc.
(admin. by BMG Music Publishing)/Greg Nelson Music (admin. by The Copyright Company).
All rights reserved. International copyright secured. Used by permission.

Hiding Place

**Words and Music by
STEVEN CURTIS CHAPMAN
and JERRY SALLEY**

© 1987 Sparrow Song (A div. of The Sparrow Corp.) and Careers - BMG Music Publishing, Inc.
(admin. by Careers - BMG Music Publishing, Inc.)/Greg Nelson Music (admin. by The Copyright Company)/
Cholampy Music (admin. by BMG Music Publishing).
All rights reserved. International copyright secured. Used by permission.

Run Away

Words and Music by
STEVEN CURTIS CHAPMAN

1. Strol-ling past temp-ta-tion av-e-nue, Oo,
2. comes a time when you must stand and fight, you've got-ta

© 1987 Sparrow Song (A div. of The Sparrow Corp.) and Careers - BMG Music Publishing, Inc.
(admin. by Careers - BMG Music Publishing, Inc.)/Greg Nelson Music (admin. by The Copyright Company).
All rights reserved. International copyright secured. Used by permission.

His Eyes

Words by STEVEN CURTIS CHAPMAN
and JAMES ISAAC ELLIOTT

Music by STEVEN CURTIS CHAPMAN

Freely

1. Some-
times His eyes were gentle and filled with laughter, and sometimes they cried.
times His voice comes calling like rolling thunder, or like driving rain.

Sometimes there was a fire of holy anger in
And sometimes His voice is quiet and we start to wonder if He

© 1988 Birdwing Music/Sparrow Song (Divisions of The Sparrow Corp.) and BMG Songs, Inc/Careers-BMG Music Publishing, Inc.
(admin. by BMG Music Publishing)/Greg Nelson Music (admin. by The Copyright Company).
All rights reserved. International copyright secured. Used by permission.

My Turn Now

Words and Music by
STEVEN CURTIS CHAPMAN
and BRENT LAMB

© 1988 Sparrow Song (A div. of The Sparrow Corp.) and Careers - BMG Music Publishing, Inc.
(admin. by Careers - BMG Music Publishing, Inc.)/Greg Nelson Music (admin. by The Copyright Company)/
Singspiration Music (admin. by The Benson Company).
All rights reserved. International copyright secured. Used by permission.

His Strength Is Perfect

More To This Life

Words and Music by
STEVEN CURTIS CHAPMAN
and PHIL NAISH

© 1989 Sparrow Song (A div. of The Sparrow Corp.) and Careers - BMG Music Publishing, Inc./Beckengus Music and BMG Songs, Inc.
(admin. by BMG Music Publishing)/Greg Nelson Music and Pamela Kay Music (admin. by The Copyright Company).
All rights reserved. International copyright secured. Used by permission.

I Will Be Here

Words and Music by
STEVEN CURTIS CHAPMAN

© 1989 Sparrow Song (A div. of The Sparrow Corp.) and Careers - BMG Music Publishing, Inc.
(admin. by Careers - BMG Music Publishing, Inc.)/Greg Nelson Music (admin. by The Copyright Company).
All rights reserved. International copyright secured. Used by permission.

Love You With My Life

Words and Music by
STEVEN CURTIS CHAPMAN

© 1989 Sparrow Song (A div. of The Sparrow Corp.) and Careers - BMG Music Publishing, Inc.
(admin. by Careers - BMG Music Publishing, Inc.)/Greg Nelson Music (admin. by The Copyright Company).
All rights reserved. International copyright secured. Used by permission.

Treasure Island

Words and Music by
STEVEN CURTIS CHAPMAN

© 1989 Sparrow Song (A div. of The Sparrow Corp.) and Careers - BMG Music Publishing, Inc.
(admin. by Careers - BMG Music Publishing, Inc.)/Greg Nelson Music (admin. by The Copyright Company).
All rights reserved. International copyright secured. Used by permission.

82

For the Sake of the Call

Busy Man

Words and Music by
STEVEN CURTIS CHAPMAN

© 1990 Sparrow Song (a div. of The Sparrow Corp.) and Careers-BMG Music Publishing, Inc.
(admin. by Careers-BMG Music Publishing, Inc.)/Greg Nelson Music (admin. by The Copyright Company).
All rights reserved. International copyright secured. Used by permission.

100

What Kind of Joy

Words and Music by
STEVEN CURTIS CHAPMAN

© 1990 Sparrow Song (A div. of The Sparrow Corp.) and Careers - BMG Music Publishing, Inc.
(admin. by Careers - BMG Music Publishing, Inc.)/Greg Nelson Music (admin. by The Copyright Company).
All rights reserved. International copyright secured. Used by permission.

The Great Adventure

Words by STEVEN CURTIS CHAPMAN
and GEOFF MOORE
Music by STEVEN CURTIS CHAPMAN

© 1992 Sparrow Song (A division of The Sparrow Corp.) and Careers - BMG Music Publishing, Inc./
Peach Hill Songs/Starstruck Music (a division of Forefront Communications Group, Inc.).
All rights on behalf of Sparrow Song and Peach Hill Songs administered by Careers - BMG Music Publishing, Inc.
All rights reserved. International copyright secured. Used by permission.

Go There With You

Don't Let the Fire Die

Words and Music by
STEVEN CURTIS CHAPMAN

© 1992 Sparrow Song (A div. of The Sparrow Corp.) and Careers - BMG Music Publishing, Inc./Peach Hill Songs.
All rights on behalf of Sparrow Song and Peach Hill Songs administered by Careers - BMG Music Publishing, Inc.
All rights reserved. International copyright secured. Used by permission.

135

Still Called Today

Words and Music by
STEVEN CURTIS CHAPMAN

© 1992 Sparrow Song (A div. of The Sparrow Corp.) and Careers - BMG Music Publishing, Inc./Peach Hill Songs.
All rights on behalf of Sparrow Song and Peach Hill Songs administered by Careers - BMG Music Publishing, Inc.
All rights reserved. International copyright secured. Used by permission.